Confessions

Confessions

Poems by

Carolina Maine

Angoor Press

Denver

© 2010 by Carolina Maine

All rights reserved. No part of this publication may be reproduced or transmitted in any form by any means, electronic or mechanical, including photocopying, recording, or any information storage and retrieval system, without permission, in writing, from the publisher, except in the case of brief quotations embodied in critical articles or reviews.

ISBN: 978-1-936686-00-1

Cover Art: An original arrangement (by Carolina Maine) of Michelangelo's sculpture, *Night*. Original source listed in a registry of works in the public domain.

TM

Angoor Press, LLC Logo Copyright 2010 May not be reproduced without permission or used for any business or personal purpose. Trademark intention to file 2011-2012.

Angoor Press, LLC

www.angoorpress.com

Printed in the United States of America

Acknowledgments

Thanks be to G-d for sharing with me the intimacy, compassion, empathy, and courage of Christ and for plucking me from the sufferings contained within *Confessions*.

I would like to thank my husband and children for their love, support, and steadfast presence in my life.

Special thanks; I would like to extend to Father John Hay for baptizing and confirming me into the Roman Catholic Church. If he had turned me away, I probably would not have the fulfillment of grace through the sacraments that I now cherish and enjoy.

To my father, Roy Blasingame, to Paul Maine Rilling, to my sister, Diana Holloway, and to all of the family and friends who love me despite the imperfections I possess-I would like to say:

Thank you and I love you all!

Contents

Wasteland

Wasteland Full 3
THREADBARE 4
Wasteland Align 5

Seeming Insanity

Brink of Normalcy 9
BALANCE 10
Grey 11
Perfunctory Life 12
JETTISON 13
Dim 14

Observations

Lingering Light 17
LIFE IS FLEETING 18
The Time is Now 20
Leaves of Life 21
THIS FRIEND OF MINE 22
These Hands of Yours 23

Observations continued...

Old Man 24
How, do you do? 25
Road 27

A Find Is A Mystery 28

Death

Eyes Blue, Grey with Elder 31
The dying Hour 33
Grief 34

Wanderer

How to Love 37
Intimacy of this Affair 38
Kindness Can Consume 39

The Haunted Forest 40
Raw Emotion 42
Eyes of Dawn and Dusk 43

Captain 44
Sparse Barren 45
She Buried Him 46

Wake

Dawn	49
Dawn, A Companion	50
Epiphany	51
Magnificent Tonal Array	52
Numbness of Body	53
Wondering Reign	54
Scenery	55

Nettle Songs before conversion…

Be Not Unkind	59
Covenantal Love	60
Floating	61
Laughing	62
Love	63
Fortunate Starvation	64
When Upon Ill Fate	66

Outpours the Holy Spirit upon baptism and confirmation (2009)...

Serenity 71
INTIMACY 72
Rose.. 73
Unspoken 75

In Repose

Dim Ecstasy... 79
MY AGING BODY 82
Death 85

Appendix

The Didact and The Abecedarian. A Play in One Act 91
Portrait of Carolina Maine as a young woman.

Wasteland

WASTELAND FULL

Wasteland is empty

But full in grief and love

Where darkness gives way to light

Where time absolves all pain

Pain from guilty betrayal

Of vows said in haste

And in youth

Wasteland is empty

But is now full

Life teeming

With honesty and integrity's approval.

THREADBARE

In pain I feel

To be unraveled and exposed

Threadbare to a world—

With scrutiny far past my threshold

How then—will I survive?

The ugliness that does to me—chide

When only honesty—

In my heart—thrives

If I be of miniature sort

May I then suffer this blow?

That will not touch

My crouched form as it clutches

The earth's salty and dusty floor.

WASTELAND ALIGN

Wasteland

Serenity dispossessed

    Where absence begets grief

    And longing challenges relief

Idle living

Forced into stalled loving

    Lingering with motion's consent

    Halting with cessation's lament

Heart renderings of ache

Can never allow intimate escape

    The human form drawn

    Near exhaustion in circumference's lawn

In circle's design

Body contorted into primal align

    No comfort this day shall be known

    For love has from this wasteland withdrawn

        And absence has forevermore's seedlings sown.

Seeming Insanity

BRINK OF NORMALCY

Seeming insanity

Brink of normalcy

No void of more vacuum

Than withdrawn presence

Mightily undeniable

A pen that cannot rest

Will ramble into

Wretched grief-stricken bliss

BALANCE

To Balance

Is to sway most frantic

No stillness in its maintenance

Only static and chaotic notions—mechanic

To balance

Is to sway

To grapple

Bend

Yield

Make way

To balance

Is to master

The composition—of chaos

      And its illusory dominance

GREY

I have had days

That melt into hours

Hours of living in grey

Grey hours of loneliness

Barren fields could never compare

To the feelings of earthen bare

That I know

Without depths shallow

PERFUNCTORY LIFE

When sadness comes

It drives away passions

Life becomes perfunctory

Restless no more—is my heart

Listless—it barely beats

Never stirs—for more impassioned feats

When melodies operatic do sound

Slight inner wakes do compound

But heart laden—broken

Isn't worth torturing—for token

Gestures given only in haste

When time and love

Forever remain chaste

JETTISON

Travel
To travel
To leave
To jettison
This human shell
Into—
An exotic locus
I do fancy
But I am here
In this predicament
This solitary
Confining prison
The walls of home
The sun of possibilities teasing me
Through dusty blinds binding
My view of the world
That I must visit
Without
External
Bodily
Participation

DIM

Dim is the mind

Mine

Unfound

And forgotten

I left it long ago

Amid wanderings to and fro

Places I should never have tread

A hell of my own invention

And consequent invoked deception

Do I wish to remain?

In the dim of this realm

Verily,

I do not

If more understanding

Leaves me a leper

And—

An oddity among men

Observations

Lingering Light

Were these longer days, I would have the evenings

To walk and enjoy the lingering light

of the sun that never wants the earth to turn completely away

But the earth does turn

And days melt into the blackness of night

But right before that happens

Lingering light remains

And it is softer

Than even the gentlest of rains.

Life is Fleeting

Life is Fleeting?

I think it not.

Life is of no forward or backward motion

Nor is it a time—at all.

Time is not life

And life is not time

Both are distinct—

With time being, merely man- made

How may this be—no life of time and no time of life?

Simple.

As if one should even ponder it—

Life is fleeting in that the human sense of time is centralized and brief.

One cannot know another's life and must measure it according to limited, physical sense.

However, man's sense does not render life subject to human time.

Life is bound

In universal stagnation

Life is neither past nor present nor future—

It merely is—

One's birth is of a past, present and future consequence

As are the days spent living

And surely death is of no real future as it is a given—upon birth.

What madness do you suppose I speak?

To implicate life without a direction, purpose, or feat.

But truth is also as it is

And life is of the same consequence

Life merely Is

No time does it consume or project

Life is

the constant
germinating, perpetuating, and weeding out variables—us

And time is of our own—

variable rate.

THE TIME IS NOW

The time is now

And no beginning shall ensue

As *It* has begun
With mere recognition

What do you suppose I purport?

That *It* is of animation given

With thought and mere recognition

But in truth *It* is

As all things are

A knowledge one may not unlearn

Though one may, in vain—try

As sure as tomorrow will dawn or no

It is to inside—grow

Until later action corresponds with complement

And manipulation of organism's environment

follows suit.

LEAVES OF LIFE

When leaves of time
Pass into colors sublime

Death is eminent
Though the showing—a detracting sign

Eyes of wonder
Will those witnesses posses
For grandeur and beauty
Could never be between death's hands—pressed

Only when the attention from spectacle has been returned
Will the leaves plummet—a fall of necessity's spurn

A burial of ejection do they face
Only to be trodden
Beneath our feet
And worn into torn, mangled, and color soured disgrace

THIS FRIEND OF MINE

This friend of mine

I look at him

He looks at me

His mouth utters what my heart wants to hear

His actions mimic the game he knows I fear

How may I know?

Yet not understand

As I wrap my arms about him

And feel his emptiness

Yet I am drawn

As a concentration gradient must disperse

To give myself

To the emptiness

That will render

My soul—

a spiritual death.

THESE HANDS OF YOURS

These hands of yours

Fragile and soft

Belong to the heart

You refuse to allow

To grow within you

And choke the world's vine

Creeping and winding

Blooming and choking

The very beauty of your soul.

OLD MAN

The old man's eyes are grey
Blue with weary decay

He finds his hands occupied
With the warm mug inside
Palms of years he's spent denying
Denying his own—reasons for lying

Not the clean brisk morning air
Not the birds chanting bitter sweet despair
Not even the tingling of his feet—blood never pooling there
Can distract his eyes—Grey-Blue of inward stare

The table of iron wrought
Mangled into artistic form some artist thought
Would enchant a purchaser—once bought
Is where the old man sits—warm mug between palms pressed

Where is he?
Does he even know?
Has he found himself—amid his lies?

Found where his brokenness most intimately resides

His suit of distinction draped
Over shoulders of powerful breadth—earthen scraped
I watch him inwardly seek
Answers to questions— of which he would never outwardly speak

Long are his fingers—clasped
Not too tight— nor limply overlapped
Mindful of reticent's form
He sits without realizing expression's resistance to conform.

HOW, DO YOU DO?

You've been thinking

An awful lot—without blinking

Do you suppose anyone has noticed?

Your placid expression

Most precocious

Perhaps not

Most ascribe dormancy

To misfortune's lot

But I am not convinced

Of such a simple illusion

As what may seem

Of exteriors

While the mind

Inside—thinks

Not like the eyes

Whose focus

Sees nothing

But blurry

And faint recognition

Of all who judge

And leave

Without asking

"How, do you do?"

For those in nursing homes

ROAD

I have walked this road before

In times of summer

Now fall has come with its wanderlust

And has settled upon the days

Falling, the leaves are floating

Down to the earth

Rather than flitting up toward the heavens

This road

I have walked it before

When it was lush from spring's retreat

Full with summer's heat

Now leaves falling and twirling down

Toward the earthen road

Worn only

Where I and others have trodden.

A FIND IS A MYSTERY

A find is a mystery

A beginning into

Another life—one—never before looked into

Finding another

Is a beginning of two

Another life or knowing

A kind of in—to

An inner realm

Of mutual exploration

An ordinary day's deliberate—and ecstatic—deviation

A find is a new

A searching of two

And life is anew

When lovers meet—and delve below the glimpse—of in-to

Death

EYES BLUE, GREY WITH ELDER

Eyes blue

Grey with elder

Hiding beneath lenses—finger print laden

I see you

And though you change

As my does my age

Your face never leaves

As memories rewind and shutter forward

At my will—or upon smelling

kitchen smells—fried chicken—apple turnovers

or sounds—like the early percolator—

 from which I was too young to sip

or lessons—when you taught me to peel a tomato

I confess—I had almost forgotten

Until age found me searching how to accomplish

peeling the tomato that I remembered—faintly—how to do

All because of you

I love memories-- they are my only journal

They define me and make me a Life

A life that you have nurtured

And so I

Have grown to love

You as though I had known you

Before I came along

And I will ever

As I age and grow elder

I shall peek from behind finger print laden lenses

With eyes blue

Grey with elder

As a tribute

To my love and appreciation—for you.

For my late grandmother, Mrs. Nona Fuller.

THE DYING HOUR

If you could find the dying hour
Where the willow devours
The landscape's open view
Would you then have found

Where man must rest
Laid or sprinkled
A common ground

If all is to disintegrate
Disassemble and rot into disassociate

Why must life spring into fashion?
Weld and cling-- manifest visceral association

If to fashion is to disassemble
Why must G-d punish those with destructive selves?

GRIEF

Grief rides emotions,
On swells of time, forlorn.
In heaves of forced existence,
The body works against the universe's crushing weight.

Imperceptible to those who witness,
The afflicted's placid countenance,
For, the mark of grief is a subtle show,
Its metastatic wrath taking place within the heart most below.

Grief of the core is most unkind,
It destroys the elemental construction of human being,
Though it leaves wakes,
Through which faintness begins delicate invasion.

A faintness—a peace of time,
Time of another form,
That of a soothing medicinal balm.

Within the hours of destructive grief,
The body most afflicted succumbs,
Yet grief fails in destructive mission,
 For, savior peace is the heart's champion—won.

Wanderer

How to Love

There are times when you don't know how to love
When you doubt your ability to allow vulnerability

Times when anger colors the soul dark—
Clings to the viscera creating an unwillingness to embark
Venture out into inner submission to another

In solace, grieving pain does grip
The heart that is paralyzed from fear's icy dip

Willingness—the step taken back
Clumsy footing—wobbling from emotions distraught

This soul caught
In fear's webs held taut

A mess of me has love made
Now all I ever wanted—I find from which—I long to fade

In asking why—
No answer from this place most shy

But perhaps it is most limpid—why

So afraid

That fragile love might die

INTIMACY OF THIS AFFAIR

Time in this

Allows intimacy of this affair

Yet, I am of sorrow's weakened sort

And fathom not,

    This mutual embrace

And leave it for—another's Face.

Kindness can consume

Kindness can consume

Hearts longing to assume

Positions more than humanity's doom

    For in this mourning

    One must weep

    For another

    Instead of one's keep

Life must resume

Despite death that doth consume

The heart of liars

Such

That loving becomes destructive

As much

When known are these

The soul does freeze

    For the mind may never control

    The heart that steered

    Without control

The Haunted Forest

I once wandered into a magnificent glen

With soles of blood and sin

    During the foray

    I did find

    Myself and all

    My sorrows did subside

In symbiotic sway we did lie

Upon the violent earth

Just the sheltering glen and I

    Marauders and bandits did multiply

    Yet I remained in the glen

    For I

    Became its "kept"

No bandit could me from it pry---

    Foolishly though I must confess

    Upon entrance

    I signed a waiver in most distress

If ever the deed holder should return…

I must abandon my dwelling home.

Verily, it did happen

The deed holder did return

Found me contemptible—

 and from the glen I was spurned

Scrambling in jostled painful mass

Trying to recover the integrity I had once amassed

I linger here remembering with frail form

The sweetest days of now joyful mourn

Though I was ejected

Dropped without sympathetic care

I find myself in solemn stare

Wondering how

If ever

I was special there

RAW EMOTION

Sadness

Raw emotion

The swells of longing and failed devotion

Lovers' quarrels of worldly episodic commotion

The exhaustion

Of living in a soul

Tormented by its very inability to console

Itself into peaceful lull

In order to sleep this night

Without eyes tears full

Eyes of Dawn and Dusk

Sad, eyes that pour like salt cans,
Into raw wounds of regret.
Fearful that another word will exacerbate,
The pain only a weeping songbird may imitate.

Of days that never ran,
Of love that was spoken only to be denied,
Sad, eyes that hurt from the glare of life's scorn,
Find helplessness and retreat in wounded form.

Wounds of days never spent,
Hours missed and kisses lost,
Pictures of memory—no keepsakes of the material,
Only internal paintings of memories both genuine and created.

Love, reddens the sad eyes that pour,
With salt that stings the body and the mind,
No dawn in elder years will the mind fail to remember,
Love, a dusk that set without permission mine.

Sad eyes of wrenching pain,
Grit flung into them by the axles and wheels of alacritous time,
Passing me by as if I were a hopeless beggar,
Thirsting for just one more sip of love's bitterly satisfying wine.

Sad eyes of salted tears,
Eyes that will never awaken to a dawn without remembrance,
Eyes that will never close to dusk without regret,
With final heave shall my sad eyes leave, with the purifying salt of
Love intoxicating them— lulling them into awaited sleep.

CAPTAIN

I am a consequence of my nature--
A vessel of God's creation
I must participate
Within my ship's destiny
For, I am the captain
Guiding with only my sincerity
If rough waters—I must traverse
I pray my trajectory be risk averse
For this vessel of me--
Is dilapidated and weak
Too many days at sea
Have rendered me in need of repair
But I find my locus
Far from land
Leagues too far—
For my frail hope
To remain
afloat

SPARSE BARREN

Who comes with this—
Sparse barren
Like moss on a tree
Facing north--most winterly

Pine needles brown have frozen
They lay in scattered mess
The ground is ice laden
Warmth has receded to the earth's core

These days are nights
Animals have retreated to their dens
Warm is in multiples
The sole is frigid

Who comes with this—
Bouquet of blue ice
Burning with energy
That melts into formless eternity

SHE BURIED HIM

She buried him
His body was laden with garments
She wanted his skin to never touch hers again
His face was covered
His lips were blue underneath—blue from kisses that had passed
and left their death stain

Leaves crunched beneath her feet
Frozen was the ground beneath them—hard—slippery—icy
Yet his blue body was interred despite the hardness
Machines stronger than man made the hole

Her hands were bitten with chill
Motionless, she stood watching the crunchy soil chunks that
covered his box
Her mind visited strange questions
Was her heart deader than he?

A schizophrenic's catatonic state
Her own little world
Now buried beneath the frigid blanket of God's breath
The body—remains of life

Remains that will rot when the thaw sets in
Decomposition that she awaits
Frozen with him
The thaw must destroy

All that they ever were

Wake

Dawn

There was once dawn

Where awakening was slow to begin

Where morning air was moist and chilly

Where days did not exist in form…

DAWN

When the mind did not stir

When the heart did not confer

Complications that weather life

DAWN

Where alive had a flower-scented smell

Where death had never sipped potion's poisonous spell

Where the transcendental moved between dimensions effortlessly

Where the breath collapsed but never succumbed to finality.

DAWN

What it was once

It is no more

A mystery

An origami ship to unfold….

Dawn, a Companion

Dawn—a companion mine

Dewy and invigorating—the cleansing kind

Failures bade farewell as night lifted his dreary veil

Anew—Dawn's cry of prevail

> Having lifted eyes upon morn
>
> This body now not of wretched slumber's form
>
> Instead, vital and alive
>
> To challenge this day—a victory that surmounts the need to only survive

Conquer of time—Dawn's weighty might

Lifts upon the day

As gently as a dove entering flight

> Sadness, glorious nectar,
>
> Dawn's dew—a freshening agent
>
> Lifts away the bitterness of sadness
>
> Sweetness of loss—
>
> The strength of conquer—now a potion for healing.

EPIPHANY

When the mind is darkened

Swells seem hastened

Only still is the heart

Beating not— for, time is an unruly dart

Chasing its path— ill defined

Until illumination of the spirit—in kind

All is revealed

When the body is receptive to all notions—unsealed

MAGNIFICENT TONAL ARRAY

Misty humid
Is the day
Colors smeared
Into tonal magnificent array

Lake of rain droplets dimpled design
Finds me strolling the banks with linen rolled knee high
Mud of red that does bleed
From the southern ground—of mysterious intrigue

Into heart's lull
I do escape
And find God's breath
Stroking the down of my sensitive soul

In pool-eyed ecstasy
Do I wander
No irritation may drive asunder
The cohesive illumine of child-like wander

NUMBNESS OF BODY

Numbness of body
But not of heart

No devastating blow
May be incurred this night

For when soul astound
The body left in mortal confound

Weeping though it may lie
Beside the stained floor of mortal strife

It does not bleed
For integrity it remains sheathed
Despite the harm that does touch

The heart that lived to live no more

WONDERING REIGN

For the wondering,
It is all the reign
For when soul astound
It must gain amid common ground

Aligned are the wheels
Of motion bound forth
Intrepid and lithe—the dance—of mirth
Movements refined—and still no more

Have the days withered
Those times of ecstasy's endeavors
To align in stillness
A motion unknown to earth

Limpid though the mind may be
The heart reclines beneath swaying willow tree
Somber the face appears
But underneath—the soul—it does cheer

The soul that advances guard
Shall know the somber-faced mystery of internal—soul-ecstasy—

      Unfold

The gathering of life's sweetest wine
May only be harvested within the precocious mind

For the plight of those with stamina ill-defined

Shall only live
According to another watch keeper's time.

SCENERY

This all seems commonplace
This—scenery desolate
Yet—in my heart
A wake I find
As it must be of another kind
Unlike me and not of usual sort
I follow it—though it may lead me north
To frigid and harsh places
I keep keenly behind—in pace
Hoping never to offend
The guide that does lead me
Through vicious lands— with grace.

Nettle Songs before conversion…

BE NOT UNKIND

Be not unkind

    As it is most unfeeling

        Think not of yourself when grieving

Live for your children

        That they may learn from your life

And follow the One

        Who leads you in secret

The One who wipes your tears

        And kisses your forehead—to ease your pain

Be not unkind

        To those who understand not—your predicament in time

For they are of another sort

        And will find the answer at a later chance

Do not grow weary

        When the world lashes out at you in fury

Rather—bend low—and be most small

        And the world and its greatness—will blow on by

COVENANTAL LOVE

Love is a covenant

A binding of self

To the beloved

Despite

        Hardship or ill health

Do you love?

Do you find?

Responsibility for the beloved's welfare—

Prominently—on your—mind?

Love must be a sacrifice

A dripping of life's blood

Painful it will seep

From the wounds life inflicts

        But wonderful the experience

            To sacrifice for nurturance

Have you not learned?

        Sweet sacrifice—is the food of life

FLOATING

We, humans, float

On the breath of God

We have no prominence

In this universe—a tyrant of infinite might

All we accomplish are revolutions

Around a fire ball—hell's companion

We are vulnerable

Like Jesus on the cross

Our day will come

When we must endure

The realization of our vulnerability

And that we—in bodily form—represent

Universe constituents

Small—and at best—

An annoyance as detectable

As a bed of ants

Laughing

Laughter is a mark
A human intercession
A brevity of flee
   From a mind—deprived of glee

Laughing are the angels
For no resonance of voice shall diminish
The laughter—their forms do furnish
The happiness

    The glorious Presence

Humans—why do you weep?
Did not Jesus—his promise—keep?

 He bled his being
For the sake of humanity
How do you approach?

Innocence murdered by the world—despite its bearer's hopes

  Do you find its execution in those you despise?

    Those you fail to understand and justify reasons to criticize?

Humans—when do you laugh?

And when you do—

Is it alone in selfish company?

    Or—with the angels—in glorious harmony?

LOVE

Loving is done
Before it begins
As a constant has neither

        A beginning nor an end

Language fails
A perfection that lies not within

Humanity's

        Finite skin

FORTUNATE STARVATION

Fortunate starvation
This heart has lived
Despite droughts with no bounty to yield

Fortunate in spirit
This frame does maintain
An excellent source for mercy
And passion that no fulfilled heart could sustain

Lingering ache
No starvation could imitate
A hunger beyond mortal need
A desire flaming with divine-intimacy's seed

How may I cease
When my body shall be rendered beneath
The heaping earth
That is no match for my heart's austere mirth

Had I known in childhood's girth
That I would grow into a passionate being—hurt
I would have killed
The heart that would in the future strain against fury to live

Though I've been brutally thrown
From innocent understanding's belong
I am alive none-the-less
Despite death's savage and beastly attempts at theft

For, my heart is forever conformed
To that of God's—violent and strong
It will prevail
Despite soil and metered hail…

As a reminder

To those who would fail

The brutality of life

    Is a most nurturing

        And refreshing

            Ever—deepening—well.

WHEN UPON ILL FATE

When upon ill fate
One finds their journey must traverse

With only fragile pack
And armed only with solitude's nook

The body ceases
The mind limpidly increases

Breaths exit with departing sorrow
And return with pleasant grief

Love
The Love that disassembled
Worn ragged from Life's ill fate

A chance of destiny
Happenstance of one's own reality

Solidified

Immortal

Moments swelling within the mind
Grief trails with tears of gratefulness

Knowing

Loving

The loss

The death

The resurrection

Loving with internal eyes
Far more observant than those external

A glimpse of G-d now known
From the kiss of another

With all internal strife

Should one retreat or walk the path overgrown

Nettles and tears do sting
In the end

Only peace
A heart at rest
With pleasant song to sing

Outpours the Holy Spirit upon baptism and confirmation (2009)...

Serenity

Serenity is joy without color

Unlike joy-it is of a neutral hue

Taking on no vibrancy or coldness

Serenity is peace without wake

A placid body of water

Far from stagnant

But, rather, conversely

Brimming with fullness and teeming with life.

INTIMACY

Intimacy is inner soul matter

Substance of divinity

A mingling of uncertain dimensions of profundity

 To climb

 Intertwine

 Become a ravenous vine

 Encroaching territories often inhospitable

Intimacy transforms

Landscapes both interior and exterior

Fluidly carves inlets

Through which love rushes forth

 Passion

 Is not bound by circumstance or pain

 Rather

 It is released through intimacy and grace

Passion

Is the intimate in-dwelling release

Of the Holy Spirit.

Rose

There's always blasphemy in a rose given

When there's no time for appropriate consummation

Like a flicker of a nearly extinguished candle flame

Departure with blood-stained petals only poetically reinforces

The death of love that was never real in occurrence

Love is not a flower cut and shared

Denied its life-roots

Love is daily tending

From seed to sprout

From bud to pruning

Pruning that yields future buds and growth

To be enjoyed by both the rose bush and its care-taker

To be admired by passers-by

Roses don't belong in vases

Regardless of how crystal, antiqued, or royal

Given in the haste of tumultuous emotion

Love is not a decaying flower-cut just for an occasion

Love is a thriving vine of thorns

Adorned with delicate buds and blooms

Severing love from its roots

Only allows for withering of what was once

splendid and holy.

Unspoken

In kindling that which is unspoken

Silence of the tongue does not distort

That which dies internally to passions corrupt

    Love of Christ

    The healing of confession

    Spoken through mortal lips

    I fear kindness will lead to love

Not the love of passionate lovers

But rather

Love for another-a deep emotional bond

    This wound of me

    Heart ache

    Love that never truly fits within acceptable confines

Exasperating is discernment

To reveal my soul in its bare flesh

    Or rather

    Reveal it not

    Both with consequences unknown.

In Repose

Dim Ecstasy

Though I live in dim ecstasy

The moon and stars shine only for me

In love, my heart aches for them more

Their brilliance illumines my parched soul in adore

When I die

It shall be in a most wilderness state

With the revolution of man

Crushing against my front gate

And though my heart will bleed spurts of passion

My body will convulse with life's shaken affirmation

That did

I did live

And passion

A victim

A blood red tiny rose

A meager facsimile of life's grandiose

I was

In love

A lover of men

A lover of children

A lover of life

Loving that had sustained my exalting condition

In words too tiny to communicate

Love that no time nor mortal expression could navigate

I am alive

And beating with rushing passion

Life's quiver

From my own

Did produce my two greatest loves

When death happens upon me

I shall be ancient…

Finding my end

With a G-d most patient

I shall not die this day…

This day is for me

As are the stars

And the loves I have been left to oversee—

MY AGING BODY

Gone are the full and ample breasts of my twenties

Nursing has left me with two small apples

I remember when they were engorged with milk

They were double Ds and I was horrified

I thought for sure they would be stretched with marks

But they are not

They are little apples-the way they were when I was 15.

I gained 30 pounds with each of my pregnancies

I wanted my babies to be healthy

I watched as my belly swelled

I didn't fear the rippling tides of stretch marks

My belly is now as flat as it was in my youth

And its skin is blemish free

My bottom was once muscular and round

But childbirth did spread my hips wide

My bottom is now a pear

Pears are good

Still shapely-even if not round

My face is much older now

Lines are appearing around my eyes

My forehead has small creases

My cheeks are still full of awkward dimples

My lips-they are perfect

I wouldn't change them at all

My hair bleaches red in the sun

From red it fades into gold

These days steely gray hairs make their way

To the front of my part

My husband plucks them out with tweezers

My body is aging

I still find it beautiful

It has created life and nourished it

It has been my soul's dwelling home…

Until the end, I will care for it

And when I'm done

It will lie in peace

As beautiful as it was-the day that I was born.

DEATH

Death

Where does death happen?

Does it happen in the skin-across which no more wind blows

Or does it happen in the soul-a crawl of internal to down below

Does it happen with petals stinging the eyes?

Or does it happen with internal salts causing them to cry?

Death

Why make it for more?

It is what makes us lie down for prayer in adore.

Appendix

The Didact And The Abecedarian

This is a play in One Act.

The scene is Professor Marauder's office.

The office is cluttered—papers, books, and boxes everywhere.

A clock of significant size hangs on the wall.

Professor Marauder fancies himself a philosopher.

Inconsela is a woman in her mid-twenties and looks like a librarian.

This work is purely fictional.

A portrait of Carolina Maine as a young woman.

Professor Marauder: *Answers knock at the door while continuing to read.* Come in. *Inconsela enters; Marauder looks up.* Hello Inconsela, what may I assist you with?

Inconsela: Professor Marauder, I was wondering why the A precedes the B and follows the Z.

Professor Marauder: Follows the Z? A doesn't follow the Z.

Inconsela: It most certainly does!

Professor Marauder: What proof do you have of this phenomenon?

Inconsela: If I must answer my own question, why are you here for consult?

Professor Marauder: Perhaps it is a technique of mine—to invoke pupils' minds into use.

Inconsela: What a ridiculous statement!

Professor Marauder: How so?

Inconsela: My mind has been in use as I formed a valid question to present you with.

Professor Marauder: If your mind was indeed being used, you would have found your own question to be erroneous?

Inconsela: What use then—would your position be—if I and other pupils found our own errors?

Professor Marauder: Do you want to explain to me how A follows Z or not?

Inconsela: Very well. A follows Z as the alphabet is constant in its linear proportions.

Professor Marauder: If it is linear, how may you find A following Z? Does that not suppose a circular set?

Inconsela: Circular set! How ridiculous. There are no circles—only man created ones.

Professor Marauder: Very well then—linear attributes are to be as artificial as circular ones.

Inconsela: Nonsense! The universe is of a repeating linear construct!

Professor Marauder: And you know this to be true because….

Inconsela: The universe is of linear construct as it follows a pattern of elements in sequential order that when combined create matter from the matter of sequential elements.

Professor Marauder: So—are you suggesting A, B, and C are classically placed according to elemental construct rather than arbitrary assignment?

Inconsela: Arbitrary assignment is man's way of separating elements that cannot be discerned fully by limited human awareness and understanding.

Professor Marauder: If what you say be true, how then, do you expect to know the secrets of the universe and of the alphabet that not even the brightest living minds have ever been able to conceive of?

Inconsela: It is unwise to suggest that I intend more by my suggestion placement before you than I actually intend.

Professor Marauder: Then—what are your intentions?

Inconsela: To understand why A follows Z.

Professor Marauder: Well—then you will be at peace of mind to know that A has never nor will ever follow Z.

Inconsela: Sir, I mean no disrespect, but A certainly does follow Z and I want to know why.

Professor Marauder: Then I suggest you seek another source as I am unable to help you.

Inconsela: Sir, you are more than qualified to assist me, but you are not doing it properly.

Professor Marauder: Properly—me—not assisting properly. Are you mad?

Inconsela: Do you always respond to confusion with anger?

Professor Marauder: I'm not angry!

Inconsela: Then why are you red?

Professor Marauder: I simply do not see myself as red.

Inconsela: *Amused.* How then, do you view yourself?

Professor Marauder: A color other than red.

Inconsela: You see yourself a color?

Professor Marauder: I'm indeed a man of a cool shade that is sensible and willing to assist when asked. However, I am not the type of color that ventures past the sensible shades into the emotional colors.

Inconsela: Interesting. *Changing the subject.* Why do you think A follows Z?

Professor Marauder: As I have already stated, A is the beginning of a string of letters and Z is the end of that string. A cannot follow Z no more than the geocentric model can exist.

Inconsela: Oh, but you err.

Professor Marauder: Where?

Inconsela: The geocentric model can and does exist when man suggests that he is the center of the universe and all learning contained within it. And because man cannot know anything other than being man—the earth—representing the seat of inner humanity—and its very existence—may be considered the source around which the sun (or intellectual illumination) revolves. Has not modern science proven that man cannot be intellectually illumined by an imaginary or God source—but that his very own intellect can create a source and system of universal knowledge?

Professor Marauder: Surely you believe not what you suggest. Modern science has fully determined the heliocentric model to be the truth and final reality of man.

Inconsela: Do you believe everything literally?

Professor Marauder: Verily, I do.

Inconsela: Well—you shouldn't.

Professor Marauder: It has been my experience that reality is the best place to begin when evaluating truths and systems of learning and thought.

Inconsela: This reality of yours, does it keep all your beliefs neatly organized in your brain—or does it create desperate rifts in your system of understanding?

Professor Marauder: Why do you not answer your own question? I would be intrigued to know your state of understanding.

Inconsela: Very well—my system has very defined constants perforated with areas of challenge.

Professor Marauder: You overlook that our terrains are similar in construct.

Inconsela: Perhaps you are correct, but the quality of mine is of a more elegant and ornate nature.

Professor Marauder: I take pride in the fact that mine is of the more practical sort and am not the least bit persuaded that ornate and lofty is the path to true gnosis.

Inconsela: What is a life without aesthetic charm?

Professor Marauder: Life is a life when lived without false prompts.

Inconsela: What of beauty is a false prompt?

Professor Marauder: Just as the beautiful do age into the elderly does beauty fade into the period in which it was fashioned. But the sensible only maintains the dignity it possessed at creation and endures the charms of time.

Inconsela: How poetic of you to say such things of insanity! Do you not realize how ridiculous it is to state that beauty retains no dignity when pressed through the trends and appreciations of time? Verily, you have not witnessed the magnificence of the greatest masters of human art.

Professor Marauder: If you are suggesting that the art of Michelangelo and those masters of the Renaissance is more aesthetic than practically rendered, you are misinformed. The very beauty of their timeless forms were based on the shadings and textures of human reality.

Inconsela: I appreciate your observations but disagree with your misinformation. The renderings of the Renaissance masters suggest an immortality of the human that no reality then could substantiate. Do you deny this?

Professor Marauder: Inconsela, why do you press me? Do you not have other duties to assume?

Inconsela: Not at the present, as now, I am consumed by the question I have put before you.

Professor Marauder: But dear, I've told you my answer, and you have rejected my instruction. What more of me is expected than that that I have given?

Inconsela: Do you find that I have rejected your instruction?

Professor Marauder: Are you even going to ask me that? Have you not fought with me over the answer I gave you?

Inconsela: Fought? You think I have fought with you?

Professor Marauder: You, and I am not intending to be rude, are a confrontational young lady.

Inconsela: Perhaps I can understand why you would think that, but I assure you my intention is not to be confrontational. I seek only understanding.

Professor Marauder: You would do well to look for a more passive method of achieving understanding than your present practice.

Inconsela: Passive—Have you ever been passive about the acquisition of understanding?

Professor Marauder: Yes—I attribute all of my learning to the passive observation of the reality in which I find myself to be a participant and yet a spectator of.

Inconsela: When you are a participant—are you not active rather than passive?

Professor Marauder: No. I do not seek to identify and destroy a pillar within the framework of the reality that I exist within—unlike you.

Inconsela: Why would I seek and destroy a pillar within my very own framework of reality? Would that not be self-defeating?

Professor Marauder: Witnessing you so far, I find your very nature self-defeating.

Inconsela: Very well—you are entitled to your own observations—though they be based more on emotion than on logic.

Professor Marauder: Why do you think my observations are based more on emotions that on logic?

Inconsela: Because you see yourself as a color.

Professor Marauder: You're a bit rude—aren't you?

Inconsela: This coming from you—you who said I was confrontational, self-defeating, and basically mad!

Professor Marauder: Are you now satisfied with my answer enough to depart from this rather awkward entanglement?

Inconsela: You find us entangled?

Professor Marauder: Yes—in a certain manner.

Inconsela: That isn't very descriptive. Would this entanglement be of circular design?

Professor Marauder: Are you suggesting it be of a repeating linear nature?

Inconsela: Why do you reject the linear notion that A may follow Z?

Professor Marauder: Because Z is the end of the line.

Inconsela: Perhaps—but does not the line repeat in another dimension?

Professor Marauder: Dimension! We have one dimension in this conversation and that is the line from A to Z!

Inconsela: You're turning red again.

Professor Marauder: Impossible—I can never be red.

Inconsela: In my dimension—you are very much of the reddish nature.

Professor Marauder: There is only one dimension in this room, and I am the one who is obviously the participant.

Inconsela: Then—would you say that I am in the passive position rather than the confrontational one—since I am not participating?

Professor Marauder: No—you are not the passive one. You are the one who is trying to wreck this reality's primary pillar—me.

Inconsela: Oh am I? How do you suppose I've tried to wreck you?

Professor Marauder: You meekly knock and enter only to ask a ridiculous question—a question you know is bogus—all-the-while you are secretly trying to erode my authority and position within this reality.

Inconsela: What did I tell you about assuming that I intend more than I propose?

Professor Marauder: Oh how cleverly do you hide behind your wit—or rather—your insane sense of wit!

Inconsela: If you thought my view insane—why did you not kick me out—cast me into a non-speaking role in your grand reality that you so love to dominate?

Professor Marauder: Are you trying to imply that I have been intrigued by your positions?

Inconsela: Have I suggested such a notion?

Professor Marauder: Verily, you have!

Inconsela: How fair would it be to say that I have been as fascinated by your positions as you have been of mine?

Professor Marauder: Quite inaccurate considering that I am sure my positions have not intrigued you as you have only sought to quash them—and because I think you mad.

Inconsela: You think me mad?

Professor Marauder: Why would I think you sane—you who comes in here demanding to know why A follows Z?

Inconsela: That isn't reason enough to presume madness.

Professor Marauder: It is when it has been an all-day waste of time.

Inconsela: You consider our discussion a waste of time? Why? Because I am inferior to you?

Professor Marauder: Yes. Some minds are of the elite construct and those of a nature such as yours—cannot be a healthy stimulant to the minds of persons such as myself.

Inconsela: I see.

Professor Marauder: See what?

Inconsela: I see most limpidly that you are a helpless liar.

Professor Marauder: What have I said that would indicate that I am a liar—one who deceives?

Inconsela: You conceal your insecurities behind your elitism.

Professor Marauder: But I am your superior.

Inconsela: Verily, in some dimensions you are—but not in all.

Professor Marauder: You are not only confrontational but arrogant.

Inconsela: Are you sure you aren't red?

Professor Marauder: I am sure that red is not my color.

Inconsela: I can see that we are at an impasse. I will ask my question once more and listen to your answer—that way I will be sure to have your correct version of the answer for my consideration—for later reference. Now, I want to understand why A follows Z.

Professor Marauder: A can never follow Z because A is the first letter of the alphabet and Z is the last.

Inconsela: Is that your most solid answer?

Professor Marauder: Yes—it is. Out of curiosity, if you know that A follows Z—why then did you ask me this question to begin with? People generally ask questions when they have no answer formed.

Inconsela: You ask what I cannot answer.

Professor Marauder: Why can't you answer—you are qualified to answer the question— are you not?

Inconsela: Very well then. If you knew my question to be of bogus origin, why then did you engage me in discourse—concerning the matter?

Professor Marauder: Do you think I engaged you in this discourse?

Inconsela: Yes—I think you did.

Professor Marauder: Would you not have done the same to me?

Inconsela: No. I only remained because I am polite.

Professor Marauder: Oh really!

Inconsela: Yes—really.

A silence falls upon the two.

Professor Marauder picks up his book and pretends to be fully engrossed.

Inconsela scribbles in her notebook and pretends to be formulating a new philosophical proposition.

The clock ticks loudly—the seconds move—they do not—the minutes recognized as passing by bell tones.

Finally the silence is broken by Professor Marauder clearing his throat.

Professor Marauder: You're still here?

Inconsela: It would seem to be the case.

Professor Marauder: So—you think I'm red?

Inconsela: As red as your hair was—when you were younger.

Professor Marauder: How can you tell my hair was once red?

Inconsela: Because—it has a hue that no grey can tinge?

Professor Marauder: So you noticed it?

Inconsela: Noticed what?

Professor Marauder: That my hair was once red.

Inconsela: Yes—I did.

Professor Marauder: Why?

Inconsela: Perhaps it was an accident—your heated redness tipped me off.

Professor Marauder: Why do I have the feeling you noticed it before I was angry.

Inconsela: Oh—so now the cool shade was angry—an emotional tone?

Professor Marauder: Do you always become confrontational when discovered?

Inconsela: Discovered? I do not believe I have been discovered—or even understood—by you.

Professor Marauder: Why do you think I don't understand you?

Inconsela: If you did—you would not be talking to me right now.

Professor Marauder: What then would I be doing?

Inconsela: If you don't know—then you don't know or even have the same inclination.

Professor Marauder: Same inclination—don't you think we are alike—after all—we have these minds—these minds of curiosity.

Inconsela: But as you said—mine is inferior.

Professor Marauder: Only in age.

Inconsela: So what are you suggesting?

Professor Marauder: Am I suggesting?

Inconsela: I'm really confused.

Professor Marauder: Me too. All day, we have been sure of our positions.

Inconsela: Yes—we have.

Professor Marauder: Perhaps we are more secure in our positions presently, but have not the confirmation to advance.

Inconsela: Perhaps you are correct.

Professor Marauder: Speak to me of this inclination which you mentioned.

Inconsela: It would be to no avail.

Professor Marauder: Why?

Inconsela: Because if you knew….

Before she can complete the sentence, Professor Marauder kisses her and the curtains close.

www.ingramcontent.com/pod-product-compliance
Lightning Source LLC
Chambersburg PA
CBHW022014160426
43197CB00007B/434